MINI
MYTHS
TALES FROM ANCIENT GREECE

FABULOUS
FABLES

Ann Tatlock

PURPLE TOAD
PUBLISHING

P.O. Box 631
Kennett Square, Pennsylvania 19348
www.purpletoadpublishing.com

PURPLE TOAD
PUBLISHING

Printing
1   2   3   4   5   6   7   8   9

Fabulous Fables
Heroic Heroes
The Labors of Hercules
Mythical Monsters
Tantalizing Tales

Publisher's Cataloging-in-Publication Data
Tatlock, Ann
  Fabulous Fables / Ann Tatlock
    p. cm.—(Mini myths of Ancient Greece)
Includes bibliographical references and index.
ISBN: 978-1-62469-056-3 (library bound)
1. Mythology, Greek—Juvenile literature. 2. Fables, Greek.   I. Title.
  BL783 2013
  292.13—dc23
                                                                    2013936504

eBook ISBN: 9781624690570

ABOUT THE AUTHOR: Ann Tatlock is author of ten novels. Her works have received numerous awards, including the Silver Angel Award for Excellence in Media and the Midwest Book Award. Tatlock lives in the Blue Ridge Mountains of Western North Carolina with her husband, daughter, three Chihuahuas, and a guinea pig named Lilly.

PUBLISHER'S NOTE: The mythology in this book has been researched in depth, and to the best of our knowledge is correct. Although every measure is taken to give an accurate account, Purple Toad Publishing makes no warranty of the accuracy of the information and is not liable for damages caused by inaccuracies.

Printed by Lake Book Manufacturing, Chicago, IL

CONTENTS

Hello there! . . . 'Lo there! . . . there! . . . there!

Have you ever heard an echo and wondered what it was? Listen to the story of Echo.

Echo was a nymph who talked and talked because she loved the sound of her own voice. She was a servant of Zeus, king of all the gods on Mount Olympus.

Because Zeus enjoyed the beautiful nymphs, he often joined them in the valley where they played. But Zeus had a wife named Hera who was very jealous whenever he spent time with the dainty nymphs.

One day Hera came to the valley herself in search of her husband. If she found him there, she intended to scold him and take him home.

At the entrance to the valley, Hera was met by Echo. Echo knew why the angry goddess had come.

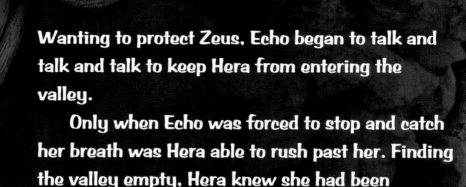

Wanting to protect Zeus, Echo began to talk and talk and talk to keep Hera from entering the valley.

Only when Echo was forced to stop and catch her breath was Hera able to rush past her. Finding the valley empty, Hera knew she had been tricked. Zeus had been able to escape.

Turning angrily to Echo, Hera said, "Because you always want the last word, you shall have it. But you will never have the first word again!"

Suddenly Echo could no longer speak. She could only repeat the last words of what somebody else said. Echo grieved so deeply that she faded away. Finally, all that was left of her was a tiny voice that repeated the last words of others.

So whenever you hear an echo, remember—don't talk so much that people grow tired of listening to you!

NARCISSUS
THE BOY WHO LOVED HIMSELF

Have you ever seen a narcissus flower bloom and wondered where it came from? Listen to the story of Narcissus.

Narcissus was an unusually handsome young man. Many young maidens were in love with him, but he rejected them all as not being good enough for him.

Narcissus was hunting in the forest when he passed by a tree where the beautiful nymph, Echo, was resting. When Echo saw him, she fell deeply in love with him, too. At this time, Echo had fallen under the curse of Hera, but she hadn't yet disappeared. She worked up the courage to show herself to Narcissus with the hope that he would love her back.

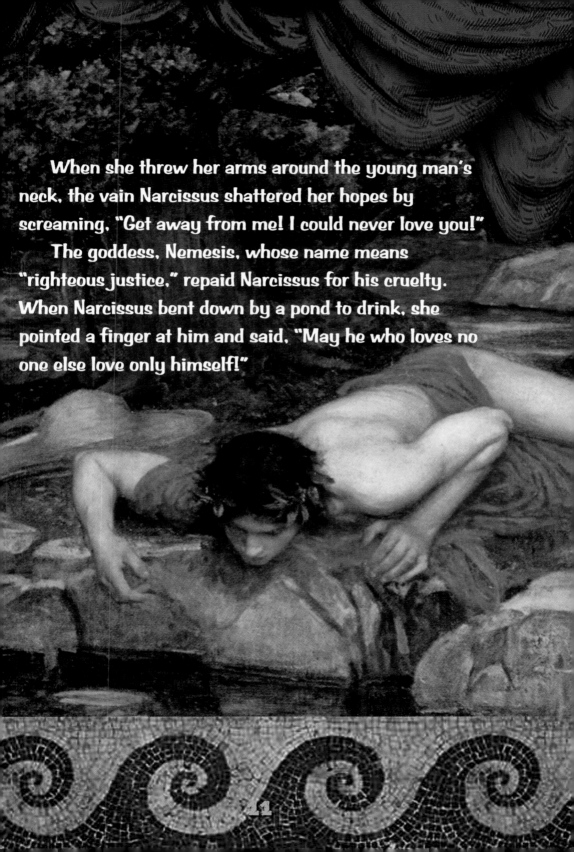

When she threw her arms around the young man's neck, the vain Narcissus shattered her hopes by screaming, "Get away from me! I could never love you!"

The goddess, Nemesis, whose name means "righteous justice," repaid Narcissus for his cruelty. When Narcissus bent down by a pond to drink, she pointed a finger at him and said, "May he who loves no one else love only himself!"

When Narcissus saw his own reflection in the pond, he fell in love with it. He wanted to touch and hold his reflection, but no matter how hard he tried, he could not do it. Still, he couldn't bear to leave it. He stopped eating and drinking and finally wasted away until he died.

A beautiful flower bloomed in the place where he died—a golden trumpet surrounded by white petals. The flower was named *narcissus* after the poor young man who loved only himself.

So whenever you see a narcissus, remember—you should always show love and kindness to others.

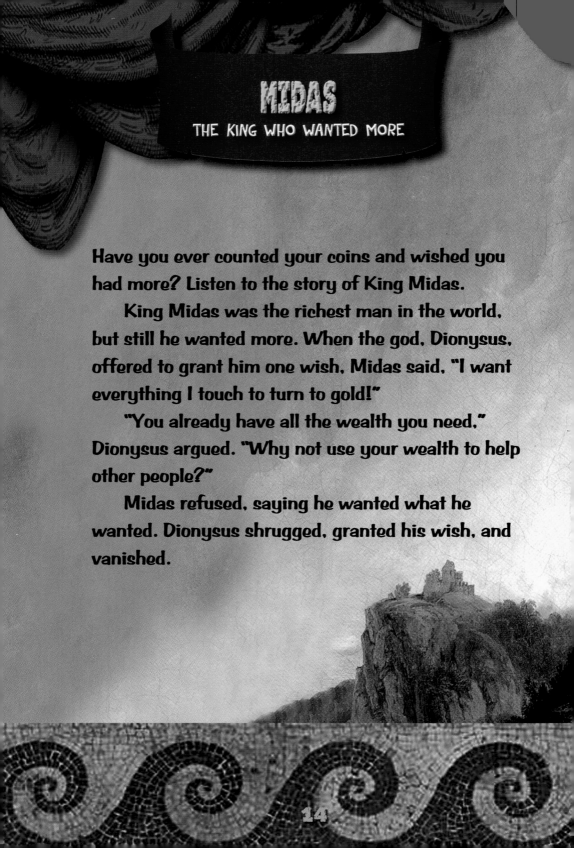

MIDAS
THE KING WHO WANTED MORE

Have you ever counted your coins and wished you had more? Listen to the story of King Midas.

King Midas was the richest man in the world, but still he wanted more. When the god, Dionysus, offered to grant him one wish, Midas said, "I want everything I touch to turn to gold!"

"You already have all the wealth you need," Dionysus argued. "Why not use your wealth to help other people?"

Midas refused, saying he wanted what he wanted. Dionysus shrugged, granted his wish, and vanished.

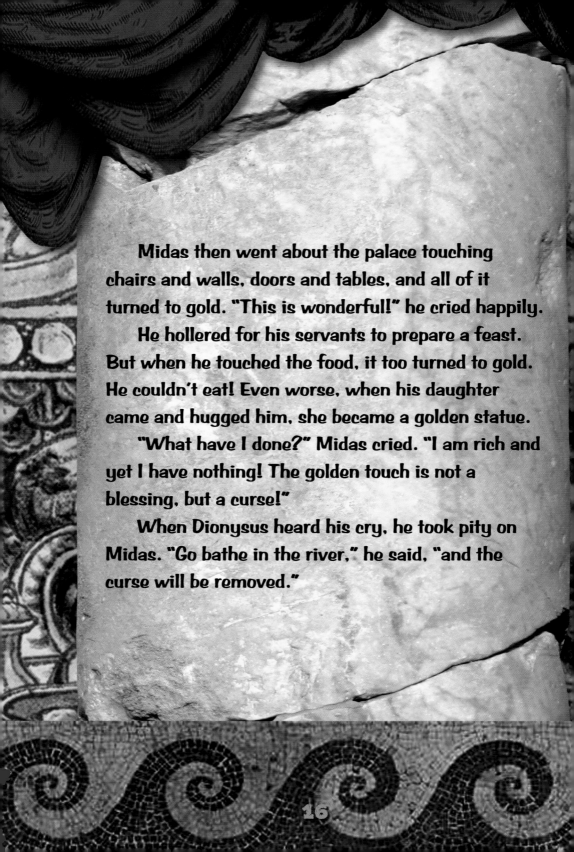

Midas then went about the palace touching chairs and walls, doors and tables, and all of it turned to gold. "This is wonderful!" he cried happily.

He hollered for his servants to prepare a feast. But when he touched the food, it too turned to gold. He couldn't eat! Even worse, when his daughter came and hugged him, she became a golden statue.

"What have I done?" Midas cried. "I am rich and yet I have nothing! The golden touch is not a blessing, but a curse!"

When Dionysus heard his cry, he took pity on Midas. "Go bathe in the river," he said, "and the curse will be removed."

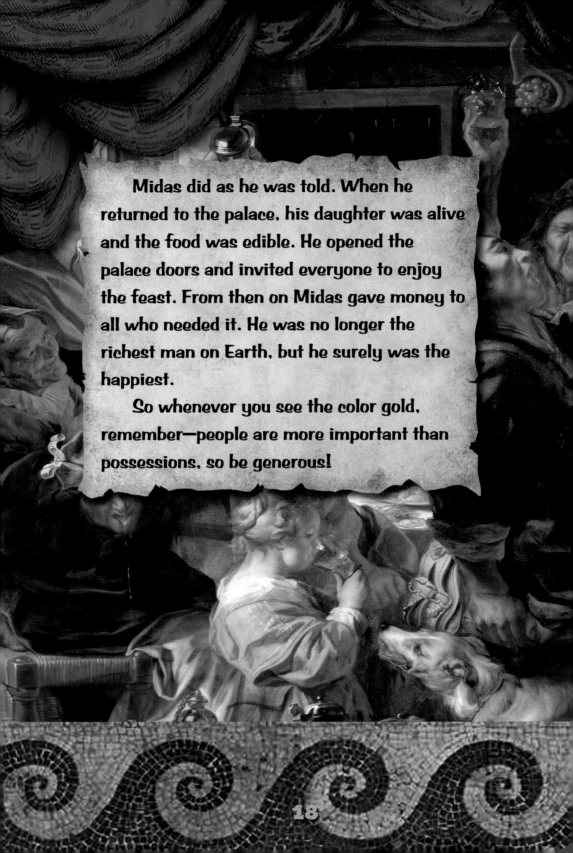

Midas did as he was told. When he returned to the palace, his daughter was alive and the food was edible. He opened the palace doors and invited everyone to enjoy the feast. From then on Midas gave money to all who needed it. He was no longer the richest man on Earth, but he surely was the happiest.

So whenever you see the color gold, remember—people are more important than possessions, so be generous!

Have you ever wanted to do something your parents warned you against? Listen to the story of Icarus.

Daedalus, the father of Icarus, was the finest craftsman in Greece. King Minos called Daedalus to the island of Crete and asked him to build a labyrinth.

Now King Minos was a very wicked man. When Daedalus finished his work, Minos said, "You and your son alone know the way in and out of this maze. I cannot let you go."

So the king had Daedalus and Icarus locked away in a tower. Every day they looked out to the sea and longed to escape. As Daedalus watched seagulls fly, he got an idea.

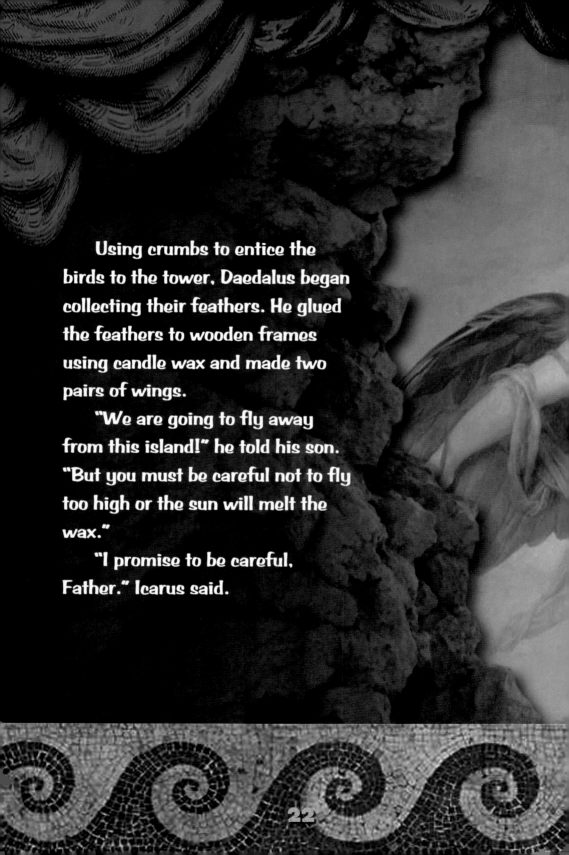

Using crumbs to entice the birds to the tower, Daedalus began collecting their feathers. He glued the feathers to wooden frames using candle wax and made two pairs of wings.

"We are going to fly away from this island!" he told his son. "But you must be careful not to fly too high or the sun will melt the wax."

"I promise to be careful, Father." Icarus said.

Father and son spread their wings and jumped from the tower. Soon they were soaring over the sea. Icarus was so excited he became careless and forgot his father's warning. Higher and higher Icarus flew—when suddenly, one feather spun loose, and then another and another, until finally he had no wings left at all. Icarus spiraled downward and splashed into the sea.

Unable to save his son, the grieving Daedalus flew home alone.

So whenever you see a bird soaring overhead, remember—listen to your elders and stay safe.

SISYPHUS
THE MAN WHO TOLD A LIE

Have you ever told a lie and thought you could get away with it? Listen to the story of Sisyphus.

When Sisyphus lay dying, he schemed with his wife to trick the god of the Underworld, Hades. "Do as I tell you, Merope," he said, "and I'll come back to life."

After Sisyphus died, Merope put on her prettiest dress and threw a party. "I'm glad he's gone!" she told her friends. "I never liked him."

Meanwhile, Sisyphus stormed up and down in front of Hades's throne. "See how she treats me?" Sisyphus complained. "No proper burial and no funeral feast. Please send me back to punish her!"

Hades did as he was asked, though he told Sisyphus to come straight back. Sisyphus promised he would, but once he found Merope, they rejoiced. "See!" Sisyphus said.
"We fooled him!"

Sisyphus and Merope lived for many more years together. But no mortal lives forever, and so when Sisyphus again found himself in the Underworld, he hoped his lie had been forgotten.

But it hadn't.

"I've been waiting for you, Sisyphus," Hades said. "I have a task for you. See that boulder? When you have pushed it to the top of the hill, you may leave here forever."

Sisyphus put his shoulder to the rock and pushed. After a very long time, he reached the top of the hill—only to have the boulder roll back down! Now, Sisyphus spends eternity rolling the boulder up the hill and watching it roll down again. It will never stay put, and Sisyphus will never leave.

So whenever you are tempted to lie, remember—you should always tell the truth.

FURTHER READING

Books

Amery, Heather. *Greek Myths for Young Children*. London: Usborne Publishing, Ltd., 1999.

Ardagh, Philip. *Ancient Greek Myths and Legends*. Chicago: World Book, Inc., 2002.

D'Aulaire, Ingri and Edgar. *D'Aulaires' Book of Greek Myths*. New York: Bantam Doubleday Dell Publishing Group, 1962.

Kimmel, Eric A. *The McElderry Book of Greek Myths*. New York: Simon & Schuster Children's Publishing Division, 2008.

Osborne, Mary Pope. *Favorite Greek Myths*. New York: Scholastic Inc., 1989.

Works Consulted

Buxton, Richard. *The Complete World of Greek Mythology*. London: Thames & Hudson Ltd., 2004.

Daly, Kathleen N. *Greek & Roman Mythology A To Z*. New York: Facts on File Inc., 2004.

Hamilton, Edith. *Mythology: Timeless Tales of Gods and Heroes*. Boston: Little Brown & Company, 1940.

McCaughrean, Geraldine. *Greek Gods and Goddesses*. New York: Simon & Schuster, 1998.

Philip, Neil. *The Illustrated Book of Myths: Tales and Legends of the World*. New York: Dorling Kindersley Publishing, Inc., 1995.

Russell, William F. *Classic Myths to Read Aloud*. New York: Crown Publishers, Inc., 1989.

Vinge, Joan D. *The Random House Book of Greek Myths*. New York: Random House, 1999.

On the Internet

Mythology Guide
http://www.online-mythology.com/

GLOSSARY

Crete (KREET)—The largest of the Greek islands.

fable (FAY-bull)—A made-up story meant to teach a lesson.

Hades (HAY-deez)—Greek god of the Underworld.

Hera—Queen of Olympus and wife of Zeus.

labyrinth (LAB-uh-rinth)—A large and intricate maze.

Merope (MAYR-uh-pee)—Wife of Sisyphus, who helped him try to cheat Death.

mortal (MOR-tul)—Human beings without divine power.

Nemesis (NEM-uh-sis)—Greek goddess of vengeance; she punished those who had too much pride in themselves.

nymphs (NIMFS)—Nature spirits, partly divine, who looked like beautiful maidens and who served the gods.

Olympus (oh-LIMM-pis)—Mountain home of the gods and goddesses.

scheme (SKEME)—To plot in secret.

Sisyphus (SIS-uh-fus)—A man who tried to cheat Death.

Zeus (ZOOSE)—King of the Greek gods.

INDEX